Life in a

By Liza Charlesworth

ISBN: 978-1-339-02793-7

Art Director: Tannaz Fassihi; Designer: Tanya Chernyak
Photos © Getty Images and Shutterstock.com.
Copyright © Liza Charlesworth. All rights reserved. Published by Scholastic Inc.

1 2 3 4 5 6 7 8 9 10   68   32 31 30 29 28 27 26 25 24 23

Printed in Jiaxing, China. First printing, August 2023.

■SCHOLASTIC

A cave is a big hole in a big rock.
It may be quite deep.
It may be as black as ink.
But there is lots of life inside it!

A cave is a home for a mom
and her cub. It's a safe place
to sleep when the wind blows.

A cave is not hot or bright.
That makes it a place for insects.
They leap and they creep.

Snakes like to stay in caves.
They slink and they slide.
They slip in cracks to hide.

Can you see fish in caves? Yes! This cave has a lake for them to swim in. Swish, swish!

A cave is a fine spot for bats.
In the daytime, they hang upside
down from rocks to doze.

At night, the bats wake up
and they take flight.
The bats flap their wings.
It is quite a sight to see!